BACK FROM THE HOG PEN

DESHAWN E. MARSHALL

authorHOUSE®

AuthorHouse™
1663 Liberty Drive
Bloomington, IN 47403
www.authorhouse.com
Phone: 833-262-8899

Published by AuthorHouse 12/16/2022

ISBN: 978-1-6655-7764-9 (sc)
ISBN: 978-1-6655-7765-6 (hc)
ISBN: 978-1-6655-7767-0 (e)

Library of Congress Control Number: 2022922693

Print information available on the last page.

Scripture quotations are from the Holy Bible, King James Version (Authorized Version). First published in 1611. Quoted from the KJV Classic Reference Bible, Copyright © 1983 by The Zondervan Corporation.

CONTENTS

De Shawn Marshall

BACK FROM THE HOG PEN

The first time I went to prison was in August of 1996. Looking through the fence covered with bob wire that surrounded the perimeter of the housing units a sense of reality set inside of my mind, when I heard the officer yell take off all your clothes. Standing there naked and afraid looking like I just stepped clean out of my mother's womb. Thank God, that I wasn't born in the time of slavery, but the picture was clear to me this day and time that my butt belonged to the *State of Florida*. How did I get here? Well, it's simple, I left the ark of safety. At the age of twelve, is when I first received the gift of the *Holy Ghost (Acts1:8 But ye shall receive power, after that the Holy Ghost is come upon you :).*

Growing up in the Seventies and Eighties under the rules and regulations of Nora Wright (aka) Grandma we lived under the rules of (Joshua24:15, but as for me and my house, we will serve the Lord). Sunday school every Sunday at 10:00am learning about God, and his son Jesus Christ was essential in my upbringing. Learning that God is love, and the fact that (John 3:16) God So loved the world that he gave his only begotten Son, that who so ever believeth in him shall not perish, but have everlasting life. At the age of five years of age I was baptized with the water baptism in Jesus Name. At the age of twelve I received the gift of the *Holy Ghost*.

The Spirit of God living in me is a feeling that I had not felt until I was twelve; with speaking in other tongues as the Spirit of God gave me the utterance. In spring of 1985 my life changed one night at the revival I made a conscience decision to give my life to The Lord. My friends all went to church at Solid Rock or Oak Grove in New Smyrna Beach, Florida. I Learned vicariously of God and the miracles that Jesus Christ performed by reading the Bible. Peer pressure was a huge fact in a little town like New Smyrna; One example, was everyone in school always had the latest dance moves, except me, I was the church boy. In Elnora's house we did not dance.

Being saved at such a young age was beautiful; I experienced wonderful trips going to church conventions all over the United States. One memory as a youth traveling from Orlando to Houston on an airline for the first time was a lot of fun. Houston Texas was brutally hot during the summer of 1985; it felt like a heater was blowing outside. Every time I walked out of the Hotel. People came from all over the world to attend the Pentecostal Assemblies of the World (PAW) Convention.

I met wonderful people of God like myself that had repented of sin and was baptized in the name of Jesus. The sight of young people my age as well as older teenagers was encouraging to see. Even though the next couple of years were filled with many trips that included cities like Detroit, Atlanta, and in New Orleans, but there was a war going on inside me. (Ephesians 6:12) For we wrestle not against flesh, and blood, but against principalities, against powers, against the rulers of darkness of this world, against spiritual wickedness in high places. Paul also said that "But I see another law in my members, warring against the law of my mind, and bringing me into captivity to the law of sin which is in my members" (Romans 7:23).

Break dancing was very popular around the time I first received the *Holy Ghost*; but Pentecostal people like me should not be dancing right? Wrong, I was dancing along with the other teens in school. One night during the week I was attending church at Oak Grove an even though I was in a backsliding state the power of God landed on my mortal body while I was praising God, and I begin to shout and dance for the Lord. That was a power I hadn't felt before even when I first received the Holy Ghost two years earlier. The power of God is so awesome, its and feeling that you just can't explain.

Later on, that year I backslid and started living a life of sin. (Luke 15:13) I decided to take my journey back into the world of sin. Then I didn't realize that back sliding wasn't a decision that I made in one day, I was already in a backsliding state of mind for weeks. In 1987, at the age of 14 one Saturday during the summer I decided I want to live of the world and be free to cuss, dance and be similar to other teenagers. (Luke 15:12-16) I desired to have my portion of the world and experience sex, among other things like selling drugs. Sean, my childhood friend and classmate knew and respected that I lived a saved life. Early Monday morning on our way back to school he was astonished when I started cussing. Shawn asked, what did you just say? Sean asked. I repeated myself. Sean was blown away at my response, I told him I decided that I didn't want to be saved anymore.

Well, you can guess his response, Shawn, said to me "I knew you couldn't make it living a saved life with all of the temptation in this world." He was right at that moment. What I didn't realize was the next twenty years would be a whirl wind of sin. The next year moved really fast, because I was living in the era of the crack cocaine epidemic. Nancy Reagan famous war on drugs campaign was launched during the eighties, and that poison was spreading like a wild fire with high wind blowing at the base of a fire. Cocaine really wrecked a lot of families from both sides of the track. Looking back now I don't know what got my attention the money, cars, or the flash of being popular among my peers.

Tru's and vouges, MCM apparel, and flashings knots of money was the style in 1987.

Before the death of my Great Grandfather, who was considered the Patriarch of the family, I really got worse as a teenager. In 1987, my freshman year in high school, I started getting suspended all the time just so I had an excuse not to attend school. Once, I pulled a knife on a bully who tried to sell wolf tickets. I also stole money from the morning store, and got busted, and got another ten days home from school so I could concentrate on more important things like plotting how to run away from home.

My homie G-Money was having trouble at home too. We were having trouble following the rules that were laid down by our parents. Spring of 1988 in the month of April to be more specific we came up with, and executed our plan to escape the strict wardens of our prisons call home. G-Money crawled into my window one night around 3:30am. The plan was to steal my Grandmother's handbag, and take the keys to the car and escape to Baltimore Maryland to find my so-called father. At the age of 14 and 16 years old what in the world do two teenagers know about traveling up interstate 95 north to Maryland? Absolutely Nothing!!!!!

Amazingly G-Money crawled on the floor in my parent's room while they were sleeping without waking them up, and he retrieved the handbag without waking them up. That was a major obstacle out of the way. Next, we was cranking the car without waking them up. G-Money and I pushed the car into the road before starting it up and off we went. I felt like my heart was in my throat because my younger uncle usually comes home that time of morning after running the streets all-night.

G-Money started out driving that night towards what we thought was freedom from our slave life. I had to come to terms that we had accomplished the first part of our getaway plan, but I was scared. As we made our way towards I-95 I had the feeling of regret, and freedom at the same time. I remember thinking did I just make a major mistake????? We found over $1,000 dollars inside the handbag where the keys were at. Flying down I-95 at 4am in the morning wasn't the smartest thing to be doing after we just stole a car. I reminding G-Money to slow down and drive like he got some sense! The feelings of regret and fear raced through me, but I ignored those feelings as we drove and crossed the Georgia State line.

Money, freedom, and a car, two teenagers that are out of control. Upon our arrival to South Carolina, we stopped briefly to order some McDonalds and pick up some rap music. What was I going to say to my Dad when I get to Maryland?

Did I make a mistake running away from home was the question running through my mind? I remember thinking what have I done, not knowing the pain that I caused back home. Once I was discovered gone with the car what was going on back home? Ultimately, G money and myself we actually made it through three states without any harm or accidents.

Distinctively, I remember around 4:30 PM the first day of our escape we were downtown in a little city in North Carolina. G-Money tried to turn around and make U Turn in doing so he hit a parked car. One hour before we checked into a motel somewhere near I-95 in North Carolina.

One thing for sure, is that I had a praying Grandmother! And I know that God hears her prayers. So approximately an hour after we checked into the hotel for the evening, we struck a parked car downtown North Carolina. I don't remember the exact city, but I do remember people looking at us as we fled the scene of the accident.

A few months earlier I met my father for the first time. It was in 1987, and I was only 14 years old. For some odd reason my Mother Joedoll, God bless her heart thought that my father could help me get back on track with all of the troubles I was having in school one of the main reasons was I wasn't able to stay in school I was being suspended all of time. It was a cool night in November as we pulled up to the gas station in Jacksonville FL and I remember seeing the vision of a 560 SEC Mercedes-Benz pull into the gas station and my Dad hopped out of the car and he said to me "what's up Jack you have your stuff with you".

My best guest he was talking about my clothes, I said "yes I do". Now my Mother, bless her heart she thought that having this guy talk to me for a weekend would be good for me, that was an erroneous thought! Dwayne or as his friends called him "Punchy" was a 2-bit hustler. He hustled everything from shooting pool to selling fake jewelry to people out on the street.

At the age of 14 being around my dad for the first time felt like a great feeling my dad wanted to know that his son wasn't going to grow up to be a man that loved other men, but only women. As a matter of fact, my father made sure that I lived the life of a grown man that weekend by making sure that I was sexually active with grown women he wasn't cognizant of the fact that he was creating a monster by getting me hooked on the lust of the flesh, and the pleasures of the flesh and even though I was only 14 years old I created sexual misconduct with grown women that weekend.

The car punchy drove was beautiful it was a brand new 560 SEC Mercedes-Benz A-2 door coupe that also had a cell phone inside the car. I had never seen a car with a phone inside of it until then! That weekend I witnessed my father win money shooting pool. I witnessed my father walk out without paying a check for lunch, and I witnessed my father sell fake jury to people. People that thought the jewelry was actually real gold and diamonds so I was getting a firsthand education in how to be a thug in this life.

First thing I did when I got back home to New Smyrna Beach FL after a weekend with my father, and being educated on how to be a thug, and to make money in a malicious manner. I called G-Money and told him everything. A plan was born or should I say a plot was born to run away from home was formed from that day forward. G-Money and myself was trying to figure out a way to get away from prison we called home low and behold the devil gave us a plan to flee from home while sitting at the Pettis Park, and while riding our bicycle's.

You guessed it by now blue lights surrounded us in this little town first they asked me and G-Money who was driving when the car struck the parked car on the side of the street; and G-Money said "I was". These cops really played it cool with us they ran the tag and then they came back with a ticket for G-Money like a normal traffic stop. Could it be that the car is not reported stolen? Reality kicked in and more uniform officers showed up, then the questions came "do you have any knifes or weapons in the car?" Said the officer! The second we stepped out of the car we were placed in handcuffs!

Being arrested is as horrible as you can imagine. Hands were cuffed and placed behind my back even though we were harmless kids the officers had to follow protocol. I was locked away at a detention center while G-Money was taken away to an adult jail in North Carolina if you are 16 years old you are considered an adult. It would be a year later before I would see G-Money again, oh because after spending four days in detention center my family including my Grandmother came to pick me up, and she said to me "you are still my baby" Did I men;on she rescue me and my mother when I was only one month old from Baltimore Maryland and brought the both of us back home to New Smyrna Beach. She rescued me again from the authorities in North Carolina.

To my surprise I was not allowed to go back home to live with my Grandmother, but my new residence was with my Mother in Jacksonville FL. It was now spring of 1988, the month of April and I was getting a fresh start in Jacksonville, FL two months before my 15th birthday. School in the city was really different, but just like anywhere there was two different types of kids hardworking and kids that came to school because they had to come to school.

Northwestern Jr. High seemed like a fashion show people really took pride and dressing and wearing name brand shoes and name brand jeans. I could tell the drug dealers from the kids who actually had jobs. I didn't care much for this school, my next-door neighbor by the name of Chris was a cool kid he was two years younger than I was, but he had a lot of street sense. I remember his mother was an addict, and I felt sorry for him, but his Grandmother did the best she could do raising him up by herself without much financial support from her daughter.

I have so much more respect for my Mom because at this time in my life she was a single mother and raising a son in the late 80s was very difficult because of all the temptations and things that were in the world at this time. We didn't have very much but we did have each other. My Mom worked a job that was a dead-end job, and I had to grow up really fast so when I turned 15 years old, she doctored my birth certificate to make it seem like I was 16 years old and I was able to get a job at a McDonald's on Phillips highway in Jacksonville. Here I was at the age of 15 with no driver's license but I was driving on the Interstate. I drove on I-95 by myself back and forth to work because I had to help my Mom make ends meet.

I will never forget this afternoon I got sent to the Deans office I got in some trouble with my teacher me and some other guys were in the class clowning around and the Dean asked me did I want to take a lick with his paddle or should he call home? I had the gumption to tell the dean no! Call my Mom. Needless to say I told him he wasn't going to lay a hand on me and he called my mother I was walking up the steps at home after school because we lived on top of the barbershop and before I can get the door open good, I saw lightning flash across my eyes how did I know she had skills like Sugar Ray Leonard. Mom caught me across my head with a two piece so fast I couldn't even duck, bob, or weave.

I should have taken the lick for the Dean at school!!!!! It was a long time before I mouth off at a school official. Al, Roland, and Chris were my new friends in the neighborhood they were really sharp guys being from the city and me being from a small town like NSB I had a lot to learn. One example was every time they came over to my house, they seemed to be starving, but when I went over their house, they never invited me inside I later learned that they went inside to eat their snacks and to drink cool Ade I was the only friend that let them in while my mother was working.

Screaming hit my ears one day I was in my room listening to music I ran into the living room to find my mom was so happy we hit the lottery my mom told me the numbers flashed across the television screen man what a great feeling. I asked her how much did we win she told me she didn't know we needed to go to the store. We get down the street to the convenience store in lower bowl we were $40 richer mom was so happy I wasn't as enthusiastic as she was! Times were tough, but God made a way out of no way for us.

Summer of 1988 came and went turn 15 years old I didn't learn a lot I got to see Dougie fresh I got to see Kool Moe Dee R&B groups, and Rap Artists so I grew up a little bit in Jacksonville with my mother. In school one fall afternoon I hear my name called saying I needed to go to the office apparently my mother had checked me out and as I walked outside of the school, she was sitting in a car with her boyfriend crying and I got in the car and she told me that my Great Grandfather Walter Guinn had died. Mom said I'm sending you back home with your Grandmother because she needs your help.

First of all, this was the first time I experience the death of an immediate family member! My Great Grandfather was the Patriarch of the family he had his own construction business and he cared very much about his children and his grandchildren, as well as his great grandchildren he even helped people in the community at church and in the streets by giving people jobs and by cooking food. Apparently, my Grandfather had been sick for sometime, but he was concealing his sickness from the family. He was dealing with cancer which ended up becoming bone cancer. He was 67 years old when he died!

15 years old now, with city slick and street smarts and I was back in the small town of New Smyrna Beach man you couldn't tell me nothing, I thought I had it all together wearing AJ jeans, FILA sneakers, and a lot of designer clothes from the big city of Jacksonville. I happened to see G money one day for the first time since we ran away and he was in the projects out in the field and he said to me it was a good plan but it didn't work!

It felt different being back in my hometown after being away for months and the way that I left wasn't so pleasant and people have a way of not letting you forget your mistakes in this town because everybody knew everybody I started school I was back in high school and I had to repeat the 9th grade over, but this time I started doing pretty good I had some of the same teachers I had the year before I ran away but I was here for a fresh start I was here to be helped to my Grandmother Eleanor.

McDonald's transferred my job from Jacksonville here to New Smyrna Beach. I started working drive-thru which was one of my strong attributes to the company. I distinctively remember working one night I was sharing my draw with a swift manager named Laura I got off I finished my shift went home came back the next day and found out that I had been written up because there was $60 missing out of my drawer when I told the management team that I didn't take anything and that Laura shared the draw with me, well you know me being a black man I did not get the benefit of the doubt!

I was learning a lot of responsibility, I ended up quitting that job at McDonald's. I couldn't work there being blamed for something that I did not do so I changed jobs and ended up working at Norwood's Seafood Restaurant I worked there for years I help my grandmother out I gave her money every time I got paid.

One year before I started working at Norwood's I got busted on the streets of New Smyrna Beach. Police was coming near me, and I panicked, and I threw the illegal drugs that I had up against a tree, and I tried to walk off, and the officer stopped me by the name of Hoover.

Everything happened so fast that I didn't even realize Hoover saw me throw the illegal drugs. I got arrested that night and I spent the next three weeks in juvenile detention center, could have been much shorter but for some apparent reason my Grandmother declined to Take

Me Home, with the Judge offering to set me free she let me sit for three extra weeks before deciding to let me come home. That was a lesson that helped me get back on track. So, I worked and went to school the next couple of years.

Next couple years went by really fast but in the fall of 1991, my Junior year, that's when trouble start again. After two really nice years of being a teenager, and enjoying my high school experience I started falling in with the wrong crowd again! At the age of seventeen I found that it was hard for me to focus on my school work. I was hanging out late at night around people that was selling drugs, gambling, and drinking! Needless to say, I wanted to be cool like my peers.

Crack Cocaine was an epidemic that took over in the 80s and was roaring like a lion going into the 90s. Determined to be cool and to show off fancy designer clothes and shoes in order to have money like other drug dealers I sought out to learn the game of drug dealing. You can learn a lot from a dummy is a phrase that's underestimated, I started learning the game of drug dealing from another teenager who didn't know anything himself. The streets will teach you really fast. People and your peers alike are always looking to take advantage of somebody that's green to the knowledge of the streets especially when it comes to selling drugs like cocaine, weed, and pills. I once had people rob me that were my so-called friends, we went to school together we played together we ate together and they turned around later on in the streets while we were still teenagers and robbed me of my drugs.

So, I made up in my mind and I purchased a handgun from someone off of the streets. I had to set an example that I wasn't going to be bullied by people that were my peers. As an example, one night I got drunk, and was out with a bunch of my friends and peers in the parking lot and I pulled out my handgun and started shooting up in the air just to let people know that I was armed and dangerous.

You want to know the trouble I got into for showing off that handgun that night listen to this. One night I'm out at the park with two other friends and we were competing for a sale. Three of us ran to a car to show the car the drugs that we're going to sale them, next thing I know shots were fired out of the car at us, and one of my friends got hit in the back. Glory to God my friend lived, and he aborted being paralyzed, and a bullet missed his spine by 2 inches.

The next day I ended up in a police car people said that they saw me with a gun and they saw me shooting one night so they knew that I had a weapon but to God be the glory I was not persecuted or prosecuted for something that I did not do in this instance the Lord saved me from being arrested that time. The Bible says the prayers of the righteous availeth much. I have a praying grandmother that keeps me lifted up in prayer even to this day she still keeps me lifted up in prayer as I am an ordained minister.

After quitting school becoming a local drug dealer and not working anymore my Grandmother gave me an ultimatum go back to school stop selling drugs or get out of her house! After weeks of her promising to put me out if I didn't straighten up, she followed through and put me out of the house where I had to fend for myself and I had to solely rely on selling a lot of drugs to get a place to stay.

Nino and G-Money what we were called after the movie New Jack City, not because we were violent, but because we moved a lot of products. Yes, this is one in the same G money that helped me run away years ago, we were partners in crime once again now this time it was bigger than just running away it was the sale and delivery of narcotics all across the county, he was on the streets just like I was on the streets so we partnered up and we started living in a hotel room together.

Two 18-year-old men living together on their own for the first time in our life with no rules no restrictions and no curfews was a real recipe for disaster! When we weren't selling drugs, we were partying and drinking going to the clubs chasing women often as we could. I learned real meaningful responsibility because my rent was due every week, even the rental car that we had the payment was on a weekly or a daily basis we drove rental cars for almost a whole year. The Dirty money was coming in really fast the only problem that I had was Gee money worked for me and I wanted him to have his own money. I guess I felt that two of us getting money together would be stronger than one getting money. I could not wrap my mind around the fact that every time I gave G money a package, he would make the money but after he disappeared for a couple of days, he always came back home broke and needed me to put him back on his feet.

Ellesse shoes, starter shorts sets, and baseball jerseys things were really moving fast; money was really rolling in and myself and G-Money were really dressing the part of drug dealers we had the attention of everybody in the city including the police! Needless to say, my plot and plan to sell drugs and to make money to show all the young women who liked drug dealing men in town that I was flashy and had money came to fruition!

Would you believe I had the gumption to believe, HELLO!!!!! That this lifestyle would last for a lifetime without any consequences! Flashy cars, and fancy jewelry, and flashy clothes we thought we had it made nice looking women how naïve were we thought the women were there for us actually it was the money the free drugs and the lifestyle that these women wanted they did not care one iota about us! At the beginning of summer things really got rolling I linked up with my partner S.T. and boy I lost a bet to S.T. I took the Lakers over the Chicago Bulls that summer Michael Jordan made a fool out of me by winning his first of six championships!

By losing the bet to S. T. I started taking drug packages from S. T. And selling them so I could make a profit and to pay him back all the money that I lost on the series that summer. Estee was a really good friend of mine we shared a lot of good times he really didn't care for G money he wanted me to drop G money from my business adventures but I couldn't do that the G money he was my partner so everywhere that I went I took G money alone for the ride even with S.T.

Beginning of Summer of 91, me and S.T. along with G-Money we went to Atlanta for a mini vacation. The reason I remember Atlanta so well in the Summer of 91, me S.T. again with G-Money went to a club on the outskirts of Atlanta GA while drinking Mad Dog 2020 and I remember distinctively when I turned and finish drinking, I saw three young ladies and I started conversating with the young ladies I persuaded these three young beauties to drive back to Florida with me S. T. And G money for a week of vacation.

We got these young ladies a room on the beach plenty of food but things did not turn out as we expected. These young women did not want to have sex with any of us unless we committed to being their boyfriend S. T. Was furious, he even kicked his young lady out of the room on the street and I would not have that S. T. Wanted me to do the same to my young friend but I would not treat her that way, so what I did I drove the three young ladies all the way back to Atlanta GA and I took them safely home. I guess there was still some Godliness inside of me because I could not treat these women wrong regardless of how they acted they were my responsibility I brought them to the state of Florida and I made sure that I took them back to the state of Georgia.

When I got back to the state of Florida it was back to business-as-usual drug dealing hanging out gambling running the clubs with my friends and trying to avoid the police. SuperCop and the police stopped me a number of times and told me to stop selling drugs. Looking back I appreciate SuperCop, because he really tried to get inside of my head and show me the things that I was taught. He reminded me of the family that I came from. We are a Godly family and a praying family; did I listen to Supercop?

When Supercop got on your trail man you had to look out this guy did not play I witnessed him come from under a house to catch people selling drugs. I witnessed him I witnessed him come out of a tree to catch people selling drugs I witnessed this guy jump off of roofs to catch his man he was the real deal... My perspective has really changed as I have gotten older and the saying goes with more information you can make better decisions in life. Supercop was really trying to help me stop look at myself to keep me from going into the system as a young black man Supercop understood what it was like being black.

Even though Supercop pleaded with me to stop selling drugs I ignored his advice. Our paths crossed before when I was a young lad singing in the choir Supercop was the choir director he is a very talented singer and bass player, now he even preaches the gospel and he has given me sound advice according to the scriptures. Even though he never ever personally arrested me during the days of my drug dealing and sinful pass he made sure that I knew that he did not condone my behavior at the time of my sinful living.

People of the highest God there are people that the Lord Jesus Christ place in our life to help steer us in the right direction and with these people coming into your life you must realize these people and you must take advantage and take their advice Supercop was one of these people that came into my life and I didn't realize until later that this guy actually cared enough about me to give me some sound advice.

Right at the end of summer that year I had to cool it hanging around G money after a brush with death. One Friday night, me and G-Money was hanging out and we were getting money as usual we were running the whole night the beeper was going off every few minutes with sales, we had been on the beach side making money for most of the night while we were going back and forth to the club and then going catching drug sales and making money!

Around 1:30am G money got sleepy so I started driving I had to go Re-Up on the drugs because I had sold out earlier that night so G money was sleeping I had got a new call to go back on the beach side to pick up money I was driving by the airport when I got sleepy and since G money had been sleeping for three hours I woke him up to let him drive, just as we got on the north Causeway and I was in a deep sleep I remember some bumping and some banging.

When I came to myself I realized that we had just been in an accident so jumping up in a panic I got out of the car stashed my drugs in a nearby brush I went and sat down beside G money as we waited on the police to get there when the police got there and as I looked around the crime scene we didn't hit another car at all apparently G-Money fell asleep hit a palm tree and the car we were riding in flip and rolled the car. The Police asked who was driving and who was sitting in the passenger side and I replied to the police I was sitting in the passenger side the officer asked me to come over and look in the car when I looked in the car there was no floorboard there was ground I was staring at and the Officer said I don't know who your GOD is but you need to give him some thanks because you walked away from this, actually you could have been cut in half. I could have been thrown from the car but God stepped in and saved my life.

DESHAWN E. MARSHALL

IMPOSTORS

Many are called but few are chosen! In the fall of 1991, I met my first wife in high school. I've been married three times and I am here to tell you that the third time is truly the charm! There comes a time in a man's life and also in a woman's life we will make choices about who we let in our lives whether it's a lover whether it's a friend or even family. Whoever we decide to let in our circle we have to be careful because people are cruel without even knowing it. The first imposter, Lisa, whom I met in high school back in 1990 when we were in the 10th grade. We shared Driver's Education class together!

Lisa picked up real fast it was like she was a natural at the driving me around town. She started watching my back as I deliver illegal drugs to people even though she was really young and she was blonde with green eyes, it did not matter my clients respected her because of me. People of God we must understand that some people come into our lives to pull you off of the path of righteousness. First time I got busted as an adult Lisa was in my life and she was my woman. When the money was coming in everything was good, I took her to see the Miami Dolphins and we did things that other couples could not afford to do. We had no children so we were young and free with no jobs and we had money to live a luxurious life.

When I got busted Lisa went back home to live with her parents, and after spending weeks in jail, I finally heard from her and we decided to get back together. I was going to get out and we were going to get married and go to work and live a normal life! I went back to church and I made a decision to go back to God and if Lisa wanted to be with me she had to follow me and learn the ways of a Christian.

As a man or woman when you start to walk towards God and your mate, your lover, or your friends do not approve that lets you know that it's possible, they are being used by the enemy, the devil. Any opposition against your movement towards God is a friend of the devil or they can be under the influence of an evil spirit to come against you and stop you from moving forward in the name of the Lord Jesus Christ!

Saint John the 10th chapter 10th verse clearly states that "the thief cometh not but for to steal, and to kill, and to destroy; Jesus said I am come that they might have life and that they might have it more abundantly". The enemy will transform himself to appear as an Angel of light or sometimes the devil will put on sheep clothing to appear as a sheep but in all reality he's a raving wolf seeking whom he can devour.

So, I left righteousness once again not only because of Lisa, but because we didn't want to remain living holy at our young ages. I was 19 years old and Lisa was 18 years old! Being an interracial couple in the early 1990s, we failed at our Relationship, I.e., I cheated on her and she was very angry with me and the one thing that I couldn't get past was once I violated probation and was sent back to jail, the lack of care that Lisa showed me. That was a pain that hurt me really deeply and I remember the words of my grandmother Nora, she said "when you have your hand in a lions mouth you must ease your hand out, you can't snatch it out!" My Uncle Nat told me while I was in jail to get her out of my system! But I was in love.

After spending months in jail, I came home and me and Lisa started communicating again. She moved back in with me and after three (3) days I decided this was not for me.

It was spring of 1994 when I got released from jail and Jonboy gave me a job working alongside him. We drove an hour each way every day Monday through Saturday and it wasn't much, but I had a job and I started really becoming a man. After Lisa and I separated I was a wreck mentally and emotionally, and for two (2) years I started dating women and being a whore monger. I wouldn't let anyone get close to me again because the pain of a broken heart was so deep. I came in contact with a lot of good women, and once I started having feelings for them I pulled back!

The next imposter that I allowed into my life was a sweet person and we lived together and I had an addiction problem. I was facing prison for the second time and I needed someone to be there for me while I was doing my time, but boy did I get a big surprise when i went to prison. She told me she wanted to move on and by the time I got out of prison it was an easy decision to part ways!

There are times that people will cross our paths and we think these people mean us good especially if you have a relationship with God, or you are trying to get close to God and people pull against you getting close to the Lord Jesus, I repeat they are not your friend and they don't mean you or themselves any good. Scripture says Matthew 7th chapter 15 verse beware of false prophets, which come to you in sheep's clothing, but inwardly they are raving wolves.

People of God beware of impostors they walk around you they sit around you everyday and sometimes it's the people that are closest to you that will try to influence you to walk away from God!

SHAKEDOWN

Growing up I really had a few good friends Bumpy Face, Supa Dave, Pojay, Wesley, and Pastor Vince, but this chapter is about Shakedown.

1995 I lost my job so hustling came easy after staying away from drug activities for a long time I got back in the game. I moved in with shakedown and we lived together for almost a year we hustle cards we hustled drugs and we hustled at the club playing pool if we could make money, we did it, if we could sell land in New Mexico, we did it! Shakedown has a real bubbly personality and he loves to laugh he can light up a room and this was his special quality! There's a game call skin it's a big fast money game and all the big drug dealers gambled at this game, I never forget one night I went in and I lost $1000 I had $40 left I took that $40 and won over $2500 that night it was amazing I couldn't wait to get home to tell my partner what had happened because we were getting ready to go to Disney World for my birthday.

One night Papa Groove walked into the skin house and won $4400 in 20 minutes we were astonished we quickly left and of course we were packing our guns with us just in case of any trouble and we got back home and he counted up the money he truly had won over $4400 in 20 minutes. Shakedown truly knew all the good gambling spots he knew all the people that had big money they were good safe people to be around while Shakedown in hustling and making money, and having fun, and eating good. I often went to the hometown to hustle just so happen one day I picked up a package of rock cocaine and while on my way to the beachside I pass by officer Griffin next thing I knew he hooked a U turn and throw the blue lights in my rearview mirror.

Look, at the time I drove a 1990 burgundy Toyota Corolla that had a lot of booms 15-inch wolfers in the back seat! I had a secret compartment built up under the speakers where I kept a 9-millimeter handgun. Now here I am minding my own business and this car is behind me with the blue lights on so I drive over to the Food Lion shopping Plaza and pulled in and I stopped the car Griffin asked me for my license I give him my license he comes back saying everything checks out but he asked me to step out of my car and he says to me is there anything in the car that I need to know about any drugs and guns and knives and I said NOOO Sirrrr, "can I search the car" Griffen asked, and I said no you may not, and he turns and throw me on the car and search me anyway and grabs my crotch and he feels something in my crotch that's not natural.

It's unprecedented what happens next I throw Griffin to the ground keep in mind Griffin is a canine officer I start running towards the grocery store which is a Food Lion I run around the back of the grocery store because I need to get the illegal drugs off of my person and I dive in the Indian River I swim out in the river I get the drugs out of my crotch then I swim back to the river where Griffin is at waiting on me what a set of handcuffs and he is very angry he's kicking and screaming after he secures me in the handcuffs he looks at the river and you will not believe the plastic baggie that I had the drugs in floated back to the top of the river, and to the shore. I was booked on possession.

I walked into the back of the Volusia County Branch Jail. I was processed and I was back on the street with me in an hour my boys had gotten word that I was in jail and they quickly got the bond money together. Even though I was out on bond I was worried because I had got arrested and I was on probation.

1996

The first time I went on a run was in 1996. I moved from New Smyrna Beach 15 miles north to Daytona Beach on the beach side is where I blended in and I was like a chameleon. I will stay here out in the hotel during the day and I would move around pedaling the product of crack cocaine by night my partner Shakedown would come and pick me up at night when we did business and we went gambling so we could keep winning money. I had what you call a runner and his name was Ali and he made me a lot of money he had a lot of clients that I did not know but I only dealt with Ali. One night I came home after being out gambling and I found out that my hotel room had been broken into. Ali had observed where I kept the drugs at and he robbed my hotel room. After a bad night of gambling, I was broke, out of money, and all of my products were gone.

After I put in a call to some friends, I was back on my feet. I had a new package of crack cocaine to sell, but here's the irony. Now that I didn't have Ali as my runner anymore it meant that I had to personally deal drugs to people that I did not know. I met a couple of drug feens that seemed really cool and I got comfortable selling them drugs. Now I had a pair of new runners that sold my product in the street. One day I'm laying in my hotel room, my hands behind my head, and I'm watching the Maury Polvich Show. I look out the window and I think to myself oh God here I go there was a cop approaching my room door.

The officer let himself into my room and immediately found my stash of drugs on top of the kitchen cabinets. I was immediately placed in handcuffs and booked into the Volusia County Branch Jail.

Marshall, "said the officer" you have a visitor waiting for you in the visitation room. They have agreed to drop all of your new charges if you plea out to the violation of probation my attorney said. It was a no brainer with all of the new charges dropped I would no longer face doing 85% of my time. I would go to prison on a 3 ½ year sentence and only do 11 months and I would be home.

I was sentenced to 3 ½ years in the month of June and I waited weeks to get to prison, finally one August morning the ride to the Orlando Reception Center came. I quickly learned that being a model inmate was the way to go home in a quick orderly fashion. Inmates were going to jail inside of prison which means they spent hard time in the box, a form of punishment for inmates who misbehave.

I was very smart and caught on quickly and time went by very fast for me. After football season was over I had only five months until I got released. I learned a valuable lesson visiting prison; I found out that the justice system did not mind giving out a ton of time; some people were there that had hundreds of years to do. I slept between two men, the one on the right side of my bunk had 25 years, and the other one on the left side of my bunk had 40 years.

I will never forget the day before I went home my homeboy was on the yard telling everybody I was going home. The next day a tap came on my shoulder, a young man that was three years younger than myself said to me, you're going home tomorrow and I said yes, he told me to make sure I take care because he was never getting out, he had a life sentence. I remember thinking to myself that day that I was going to no longer carry guns.

It was July 1st, 1997, and Return of the Mack was the hit song that summer and I was free! My sister Tracy loaned me her car for my first day home and I rode around playing Return of the Mack all day long. How ironic my ex-wife got in touch with me a couple of months before I left prison and we caught up a couple of days after I got out of prison and we hung out, nothing serious went on between me and my ex but we remain the best of friends which was a good thing between me and her and we were able to act like adults.

After a few weeks of working with my uncle Greg, he gave me a car, a classic Lincoln Town car. A few days after I got released me and Shakedown hooked up once again and while he was at the dog track he told me that our plug was ready to put me back in power with the illegal drugs. I told Shake that I wasn't ready at this time I needed a few weeks to look things over. I had to relax after being in prison it really gives you a new perspective on life just so happened 17 days after I got released my partner Shakedown was taken into custody, something about the US government not really happy with the sale of pharmaceutical drugs without a permit or a license to sell cocaine. After Shake was released from prison he came home a different man. He settled down, got married and raised a beautiful family. He and his lovely wife just celebrated 20 years of marriage.

Summer 1997 one month after I got released from prison, I was hustling because I needed money and I needed clothes. I gave a ride to a local booster by the name of Drunk, I.e., now Drunk did things that I've never seen before. He would run out of a Department Store with clothing and shoes and he will sell them to the highest bidder. This guy made between $800-$900, sometimes $1200 a day by boosting clothes. I just so happen to be the getaway driver and we were at the Sanford Mall one day and I was sitting in a parking lot waiting on Drunk to come out of the store with the merchandise, and low and behold here comes a security guard hiding behind the concrete wall and I see Drunk coming out of the store with the merchandise and the security guard jumped from behind the concrete pole and all of the clothing and shoes went up in the air like I was watching a cartoon. I gave Drunk a stern warning, don't get caught and if they get by behind you don't run to my grandfather's car, because I cannot explain to my uncles why my grandfather car is in jail so I will not stop for you. Yep these people got behind you and I told you to leave the Sanford Mall alone. Sure enough, the security guard got behind Drunk and he ran towards me while I was sitting in my grandfather's car I took off and left Drunk!

I ended up getting a job at a local garbage company. I got a Class A driving permit which allowed me to throw garbage for an hour and drive for an hour on a rotation. The woman I was living with in Deltona FL got me the job at the garbage company but it didn't last long; because I soon moved back to New Smyrna Beach and begin selling drugs.

I told myself I was going to be smarter this time not being greedy getting slow money on dealing with people that I know. I linked up with my partner Shane also known as Muff Daddy and we were getting money with cool client's, people that live in rich neighborhoods. Spring Break hit and I was selling gram sacks of powder at double the price in Daytona Beach at Razzle's night club. One Saturday

I was at the park hustling which just so happened to be February 14th, and Shane comes up with two women in which I recognize from high school. Andrea and her friend were here on vacation from New York City and we had so much fun that weekend. The girls flew us up to New York all expenses paid for 10 days the following week.

We were pretty fortunate for that week, because it was Grammy week. We got to see a lot of artists like Gerald LeVert and Eddie LeVert, Gladys's knight, and Baby Face to name a few recording stars. My first trip to New York was a blast not to mention catching up with my cousin Chevelle whom I haven't seen in 14 years.

NEVER USE YOUR OWN SUPPLY

Me and my girlfriend from New York broke off our relationship, because I came clean and told her I was snorting powder cocaine. For some strange reason she thought that I was using the money she sent me to get high off of each week. It was party time again in Daytona Beach, FL and I had my own bachelor pad and I was throwing coke parties and bachelor parties at my pad. I spent most of this year getting high and parting, Albert's house was the main spot for parting and hustling!

Supa Dave, Shane and myself hustled out of Albert's house all the time not to mention Bumpy Face showing up with different striper's every other night. Most nights started out with drinking EJ Brandy, Christian Brothers Gin and Juice were on the menu most often, and if we were really feeling good about ourselves it would be Hennessy and Courvoisier which is a more expensive Cognac. Young Dum 25-year-old who thought they had it all together, money, drugs, sex, drinking and partying was all we cared about. Supa Dave and I would often break off from the other guys to party ourselves with young women. One night we were dropping his girlfriend off and he turned and said to me, " we are about to get pulled over by the police". I looked at him, and I said, "what are you talking about?" He said to me that I just ran a stop sign. I said, "Well Dave, pull the car over. The windows are tinted dark enough. I will switch places with you because my license is good and valid." Dave looked at me with his drink in his hand his cup was between two fingers, and his index finger and the other two fingers, he pointed at me at the same time as he held a cup in his hand and he said, " Shawn, when blue lights come on, I just cannot stop. Supa said, Shawn I am dirty and I'm on probation and I've been drinking". Well you know what the police did he turned on the blue lights Supa Dave shut the lights off on the Cadillac we were driving and he punched the accelerator I started screaming and hollering pull over pull over Dave looked at me and he said Shawn if you keep screaming and hollering you're going to make me wreck, I quickly pull myself together, I calmed down and I started helping him look out four things in the road I even took the time to throw away the illegal drugs that I had in my possession as we raced down State Street from Holly Hill FL to Daytona Beach FL this miraculous thing happened the police stopped turn his lights off and went the other way I could not believe what I just witnessed when we got to Mason Ave there was five police cars across the street Supa Dave put on his right blinker he turned right he took Mason all the way out and we made it the I-95 so we went down I-95 S laughing our tail off even though I was a little mad because I had threw away my illegal drugs that was worth about $300 it was so funny. I just witnessed this man outrun the police on a high-speed chase and the cop actually turned his lights off and stop chasing us!

TRANSITION

All the partying has begun to take effect on my life coming up late with my rent not spending time with my family not going to church but always living a life in the fast lane head beginning to really catch up with me try to be careful and avoid the police was another job just so happened I was on the beach side making a sale and I had a real uneasy feeling and as I'm walking around my clients home I'm looking out the windows panic or should I say paranoid I just so happen to see a four door car with tinted windows with three antenna on the trunk and the top of the car and I knew it was undercover cops.

Unsure of myself I really need it to check things out as I drove down the street there was a shopping Plaza next to a Publix grocery store as I pulled in sat in the car and watched as I observed I saw that same car pull into the parking lot and park into a parking space so I preceded to leave the shopping Plaza I drove out on 44 west towards I 95 N heading back to Daytona Beach and sure enough that car followed me I just so happen to have bumpy riding with me that day while I was out delivering packages of cocaine to my customers.

Bing aware of the undercover cops I took them on a ride so instead of going straight to my home I continued up 95 N and I exited off at the Ormond Beach exit on you US 40 again preceded to head east towards the beach once the undercover police car got beside me at the red light, they were in in the middle that travel straight I've was in the right lane and turn right to avoid them. I suddenly made an executive decision that I was not going back to prison.

T. Gordon was my roommate at this time and he got high everyday off of crack cocaine I actually paid rent to him an I tried smoking crack myself I was hooked on the very poison that I was selling. Now I was on the other side up the drug game instead of being a dealer I was a user! Bing addicted to any drugs whether it's powder cocaine alcohol crack cocaine even peels will cause you to step out of character and do things that you normally would not do.

It was not long before I found myself in prison for the second time because of my addiction I started stealing merchandise and doing things honest people despise doing including committing fraud running out of stores with stolen goods I really D rated myself and I also found myself homeless no one wanted anything to do with a crack addict. I distinctively remember pulling myself together I got dressed and I went to church at Apostolic Faith Temple where Bishop Robert B Thomas is the Pastor and after the service speaking with Mother Olivia Thomas started speaking in other tongues and she told me "son you are going to encounter witches and warlocks out there in the streets, and that I needed to be careful, but more importantly I needed to come back to the Lord."

I really wanted to come back to the Lord but I couldn't because the demons that I was carrying inside of me we're actually stronger than my mind. The Cocaine monkey was on my back and I knew it and the more I tried to get away the more the drug called me. I even had people come up and give me drugs and get me high at times when I was trying to make a change in my life! I walked around town looking like Pookie from new Jack city but it was something on the inside of me that would not allow me to give up on life And the great thing that I found out that I had people praying for me so God still had his hands on me.

Standing outside one night smoking a cigarette outside of my grandmother's house after being released from prison a third time Pastor Hill stopped by and he told me "Son no matter what goes on you pray even if you're high you just pray to GOD and he will help you" and I carried that with me every day even when I was getting high even when things were going bad because I wasn't having any more fun out in the streets my season of running the streets we're coming to an end.

The year was 2007 and I was making a transition back to living a normal life my friend Daryl Dixon had given me a job at his company where we were selling timeshare advertising over the phone this one particular time, I remember talking to this lady by the name of Cynthia Streeter she owned a timeshare on Cocoa Beach very nice lady at the time she was married and undecided whether she wanted to keep or sell her timeshare. After gaining some dignity and self-respect back in the community and with my family the unspeakable happened I fell again started back using and getting high I met another woman that became a friend of mine but all we did was get high together and the reason it was so bad after my Grandfather, OTHA WRIGHT, passed away, I was riding around with this strange person whom I met in a drug house the day of my grandfather's funeral getting high this person they didn't even want me to go to my own grandfather's funeral. This stranger was apparently another impostor that came into my life.

December 30th 2007, I found myself back in jail. My mother Joedoll Marshall King was back in my life this time as a Woman of GOD! She fasted and prayed for me and consulted with the Prophets the word of God came that I would not be the same once I came home from jail this time.

I remember that night very distinctively I fell down on my knees and I asked God to help me, I was fighting a spiritual warfare that I could not win on my own! Matthew 11:28 Come unto me, all ye that labor and are heavy laden, and I will give you rest.

I stepped out of prison a new man, now big in working and attending church it was a process getting to God, everything that was unrighteous started falling away from my life, just by hearing the word of God every day! Once again, I met the love of my life the lady that I called back in 2007 by the name of Cynthia we started talking on the phone every day we had so much in common even though she was going through a divorce. I was a friend she could relate to because we shared a common belief in Christ Jesus.

June 26th 2010 we were married in front of family and friends an even though I am not perfect I strive to please God.

Covid 19 has affected everyone in one way or another some of us have lost family and friends I hope this book encourages all who read it that there is a savior that hears your

prayers …. PLEASE -Love a little harder hug
a little tighter and kiss until you leave a mark-
---------Lefonia Boyd

In this life we will face a lot of obstacles and challenges…
remember this one thing people will do what they choose
to do and make excuses for the things they don't want to
do-----Cynthia Marshall

The world seems that it has so much to offer, but Christ
offers so much more God is Love and he has a peace that
passes all understanding.

To God Be the Glory!

> "Some people measure success by the houses
> we own, and by the cars we drive, and by the
> size of our bank accounts: success should be
> measured by the souls we cause to come to
> Christ Jesus"

—DeShawn E. Marshall —

First of all, to the Lord and Savior Jesus Christ I dedicate this work!

In loving Memory: Walter Guinn and Effie Guinn, Sam Hives, Otha Wright Sr. Elder and Mother Sara Murphy, Mother Rose Mary Edwards, Elder John Edwards, Aunt Bertha, Uncle Foley, Rovenia Manuel, Evangelist Twain Hill, Marcee LaFaye, Boyd, Archie Thompson, Ralph Smith, Jonny Sedrick, Rita Wright, Darryl Dixon, Mother Joanne Woods, Mother Olivia Thomas, Elder Willie Carson, Elder John Lawson, Deacon and Alma Taylor, Elder Doley and Mother Teemer, Auntie Tessie Rogers Teemer, Elder Thomas Teemer Deacon and Mother King, Claude Davis Sr., Ice Cream Jenkins, First Lady Patricia Walker, Mother Rose Woods, Auntie Curlie Ann Brodus, Mother Jordan, Ruby Clark, Diane Wadley, Missionary Barbara Hill, Christine Hope, Aunt Mary, Willie Dee, Mary Lou Creagh, Eddie Mays……. You all are missed

Acknowledgments: Cynthia Marshall (Wife), Elnora Wright (Grandmom), Joedoll Russell (Mother), Tracy Marshall (Sister), Jimmy Hives, Herbert (Karen), Nat (Wanda), Otha (Ronda), Greg, Ercelle Jackie Hives (Aunt), Jaquis Marshall, Tianna Clark, Lefonia Boyd (Godmother), Carol Boyd, Maxine Cullen, Carolyn Smith (Mother-in-law), Mr. and Mrs. Darryl Ingram, Darren Carson, Mr. and Mrs. Adkinson, Derrick and Bookecia Woodard, Terry Mays, Keith Strickland, David Woods, Shane Mullins, James Jackson, Vincent and Patricia Thomas, Bishop Robert Thomas, Pastor Walter Hill, Judy Hill (Aunt), Elijah Hives, Mike and Chrissy Jackson, Mr. and Mrs. Kelvin Davis, Mr. and Mrs. Keith Harmon, Gordan Rogers, Shyriaka Morris, Willie and Harriet Woods, Mr. and Mrs. Thadus Smith, Silk, Mr. and Mrs. William Marshall, Samuel Powell Sr., and the Birdman Jimmy Hargrove.

Special Thanks To: Elder Marc Royster, and Hatti my fellow Authors!!!

Now unto him who is able to keep me from falling; my Lord and Savior Jesus Christ who is so gregarious and so wonderful! God is an awesome and ostentatious God he will show up and show out he loves to flex his muscles!!!!!!!

We continue to serve the Lord each and every day. We attend Solid Rock of Jesus Church Only under the Leadership of our Pastor, Walter Hill Jr. We have been married for twelve wonderful years. We have two children, Raymond Smith (Sasha), and Crystal Dunbar (Nathaniel) and four grandchildren, Alexia, Adrian, Zane & Adarion, and we continue to reside in the New Smyrna Beach area where we live by the Motto…

Romans 3:23 "For all have sinned, and come short of the Glory of GOD" ...that's why we believe in order to have an intimate relationship with GOD, we must Repent Daily!

CPSIA information can be obtained
at www.ICGtesting.com
Printed in the USA
LVHW101128291222
736096LV00026B/384

9 781665 577649